Bible Puzzle Marathon

Carol Greene

SAINT LOUIS

Copyright © 1996 Concordia Publishing House
3558 S. Jefferson Avenue, St. Louis, MO 63118-3968
Manufactured in the United States of America

1 2 3 4 5 6 7 8 9 10   05 04 03 02 01 00 99 98 97 96

Bible People Pyramid
Bible Men

    Fill in the blanks of each line with the name of a man found in the Bible. The first name will have three letters, the second name four letters, and so on. Your answers don't have to match the names we listed in the back.

         ___ ___ ___

       ___ ___ ___ ___

      ___ ___ ___ ___ ___

     ___ ___ ___ ___ ___ ___

    ___ ___ ___ ___ ___ ___ ___

   ___ ___ ___ ___ ___ ___ ___ ___

  ___ ___ ___ ___ ___ ___ ___ ___ ___

 ___ ___ ___ ___ ___ ___ ___ ___ ___ ___

___ ___ ___ ___ ___ ___ ___ ___ ___ ___ ___

Word Search
The Flood

You'll find the words for this puzzle in Genesis 6–9, the story of Noah and the ark. How many words can you find? Look for them up or down, from side to side, or diagonally. Circle each word as you find it and mark it off the list.

ALTAR	JAPHETH
ANIMALS	LEAF
ARK	MOUNTAINS
BIRDS	NIGHTS
CLOUDS	NOAH
COVENANT	OLIVE
CYPRESS	PAIRS
DAYS	RAIN
DESTROY	RAINBOW
DOVE	RAVEN
EARTH	SHEM
FLOOD	TWO
FORTY	VIOLENCE
GRIEVED	WATERS
HAM	WICKEDNESS

D	E	P	F	S	U	N	I	A	R	D	Z	W	Y
S	E	A	A	A	H	A	M	Y	O	E	A	O	S
W	S	V	R	I	E	T	C	V	V	T	R	L	C
H	V	E	E	T	R	L	E	I	E	T	A	R	O
T	U	O	R	I	H	S	L	R	S	M	S	A	V
E	S	T	M	P	R	O	S	E	I	S	G	I	E
H	K	A	B	O	Y	G	D	N	E	Z	G	N	N
P	R	F	N	N	U	C	A	N	S	A	J	B	A
A	A	O	E	F	S	N	D	S	Y	S	M	O	N
J	A	V	L	D	S	E	T	A	T	T	Y	W	T
H	A	O	U	D	K	A	J	A	L	H	R	A	F
R	O	O	R	C	T	W	O	K	I	T	G	O	D
D	L	I	I	S	H	E	M	M	Z	N	A	I	F
C	B	W	V	I	O	L	E	N	C	E	S	R	N

Sneaky Words
Bible Places

Sneaky words hide within sentences, just daring you to find them. In this example, the sneaky word is *scare*.

He doe<u>s care</u> a lot about his son.

Sometimes a sneaky word hides within another word: The word *pit* is found inside the word *s<u>pit</u>e*. Sometimes it takes three or more words to find a sneaky word, and it may even jump over some punctuation. In the sentences below, the sneaky words are all names of places in the Bible. See how many you can find and underline.

Bible Places: Carmel, Derbe, Gilead, Goshen, Hebron, Horeb, Jordan, Kerith, Lystra, Nod, Pithom, Samaria

1. Let the Welsh corgi lead the dog parade.

2. Those mean kids knocked over Sally's trash can.

3. If that's an order, be sure to obey it.

4. When he saw what the sergeant had done, the major danced with fury and his face turned purple.

5. She bronzed Johnny's little shoes so she could keep them forever.

6. A hole is home to a fox, a pit home to a viper.

7. "Aren't you ever going to go?" she nagged her frazzled husband.

8. We left the shore by another road.

9. It was so hot there in the desert, his car melted into a puddle of plastic.

10. My mother is the best baker, I think.

11. Although he's a fine tenor, for Sam arias are difficult to sing.

12. "You're absolutely right, my dear," he nodded.

Empty Squares
Psalm 47:1–2

Put the words from the Bible verse below into the empty squares. To help you, we've listed the words according to the number of letters in each. And we've placed one word to get you started.

Clap your hands, all you nations; shout to God with cries of joy. How awesome is the Lord Most High, the great King over all the earth! (Psalm 47:1–2 NIV)

2-letter words
is
of
to

3-letter words
all
all
God
how
joy
the
the
the
you

4-letter words
clap
high
King
Lord
most
over
with
your

5-letter words
cries
earth
great
hands
shout

7-letter words
awesome
nations

Words from Words
Matthew

God gave Matthew the words to fill an entire gospel, but it isn't easy to find very many words in his name. Here are the rules for this puzzle:

1. Each of your words must be at least three letters long.
2. In any one word, you may use a letter only as many times as it appears in *Matthew*.
3. No fair adding an *s* to one of your words to make it plural.
4. No foreign words, slang, or words beginning with a capital letter allowed.

We found 29 words. If you find 15 words in *Matthew*, you did okay. If you find 20, you did terrific. And if you find 25 words or more, give yourself a hearty pat on the back.

1. _____   4. _____

2. _____   5. _____

3. _____   6. _____

7. _____

8. _____

9. _____

10. _____

11. _____

12. _____

13. _____

14. _____

15. _____

16. _____

17. _____

18. _____

19. _____

20. _____

21. _____

22. _____

23. _____

24. _____

25. _____

26. _____

27. _____

28. _____

29. _____

Bible People Pyramid
Bible Women

Fill in the blanks of each line with the name of a woman found in the Bible. The first name will have three letters, the second name four letters, and so on. Your answers don't have to match the names we listed in the back.

— — —

— — — —

— — — — —

— — — — — —

— — — — — — —

— — — — — — — —

— — — — — — — — —

Scramblie
Words from Psalm 23

Words from Psalm 23 have been severely scrambled. First, unscramble them and write the answers on the lines provided. Then transfer the letters in circles to the lines below and unscramble them to find another word from Psalm 23.

1. CROFTOM — ◯ — — — — —

2. BLEAT — — — —◯

3. NIMEESE —◯— — — — —

4. WHOADS ◯— — — — —

5. ENERG ◯— — — —

6. STRAWE — — — — —◯

7. USHOE —◯— — —

8. PHEDERSH — — — — — — —◯

— — — — — —

What's the Verse?
Proverbs 26:20 NIV

Follow the instructions below to cross off words in the puzzle on the opposite page. Then read from left to right, one line at a time, to find out what the Bible verse says.

1. Cross off all words with identical double vowels (as in *reed*).

2. Cross off all names of flowers.

3. Cross off all pairs of synonyms (words that mean the same thing).

4. Cross off all names of insects.

5. Cross off all words beginning with the letter *U*.

6. Cross off all words ending with the letter *G*.

7. Cross off all words that appear more than once.

ROSE	UNDERSTAND	APHID	VACUUM
WITHOUT	FROG	TRY	ENORMOUS
LITTLE	COOK	GOSSIP	UNKNOWN
FLY	A	PEONY	MOIST
FREE	SNOW	AGREE	PLUG
UGLY	WASP	SMALL	QUARREL
DAMP	MARIGOLD	RUNNING	ANT
DIES	HUGE	ULTIMATE	SNOW
TRY	POOL	DOWN	DAISY

Fill 'Em Up
Bible Things

Come up with answers for the categories on top that begin with the letters on the left. Fill in as many blanks as you can. Count 1 point for each answer. If you get 10 points, you're bright. If you get 14 points or more, you're brilliant. Your answers don't have to match ours in the back.

	Bible Women	Bible Men	Bible Places	Bible Animals
L				
A				
M				
P				

Fill 'Em Up
Things Said in Church

Same directions as Puzzle 9. Count 1 point for each answer. If you get 10 points, you're bright. If you get 14 points or more, you're brilliant. Your answers don't have to match ours in the back.

	Words to Describe God	Words to Describe Jesus	First Few Words of Hymn	Christmas Songs
W				
A				
S				
H				

Words from Words
Jeremiah

The words written by the prophet Jeremiah were beautiful, though often sad. But you won't find quite so many words in his name. Follow these rules:

1. Each of your words must be at least three letters long.
2. In any one word, you may use a letter only as many times as it appears in *Jeremiah*.
3. No fair adding *s* to one of your words to make it plural.
4. No foreign words, slang, or words beginning with a capital letter allowed.

We found 28 words. If you find 15, be happy. If you find 20, rejoice. And if you find 25 words or more, shout for joy.

1. _____   6. _____

2. _____   7. _____

3. _____   8. _____

4. _____   9. _____

5. _____   10. _____

11. _____   20. _____

12. _____   21. _____

13. _____   22. _____

14. _____   23. _____

15. _____   24. _____

16. _____   25. _____

17. _____   26. _____

18. _____   27. _____

19. _____   28. _____

Sneaky Words
Bible Books I

Sneaky words hide within sentences, just daring you to find them. In this example, the sneaky word is *scare*.

He doe<u>s care</u> a lot about his son.

Sometimes a sneaky word hides within another word: The word *pit* is found inside the word *spite*. Sometimes it takes three or more words to find a sneaky word, and it may even jump over some punctuation. In the sentences below, the sneaky words are all books of the Bible. See how many you can find and underline.

Bible Books: Acts, Genesis, Job, Jonah, Luke, Mark, Matthew, Proverbs, Psalms, Revelation, Ruth

1. If you can't find your Bible, Gene's is over there.

2. I can't act, so I'm painting scenery for the school play.

3. Our pastor says that perhaps alms-giving might be part of our stewardship program.

4. To a real grammar pro, verbs are a snap.

5. Sam did a good job, but he hurt his foot in the process.

6. Mom says it's best always to tell the truth.

7. In India, a raj on a horse is a splendid sight.

8. Look at Rev. Elati on his motorcycle!

9. The mat the wind carried away is under the lilac bush.

10. A whale's tail is called a fluke.

11. We don't like this cleanser because it can mar kitchen counters.

Word Search
Joseph and His Brothers

You'll find the words for this puzzle in Genesis 35 and 37, the story of how Joseph's brothers sold him as a slave. How many words can you find? Look for them up or down, from side to side, or diagonally. Circle each word as you find it and mark it off the list.

ASHER	JOSEPH
BENJAMIN	JUDAH
BOWED	LEVI
CARAVAN	MOON
CISTERN	NAPHTALI
DAN	REUBEN
DOTHAN	ROBE
DREAM	SHEAVES
EGYPT	SIMEON
FLOCKS	SOLD
GAD	STARS
ISSACHAR	SUN
JEALOUS	ZEBULUN

```
F A H R G A D U J W M E D N
D L S A O N X K J O G E A J
N R O H D B M G O Y W H O L
N X E C E U E N P O T S B D
S I S A K R J T B O E A D X
E Z H W M S R B D P F U U S
V D K Q T E E A H A G K Q U
A L L K S N N N H L B O N O
E O U R J A N R R C E X A L
H S A A V O L F E E A V D A
S T M A E C O D Z U T S I E
S I R M S U N E K H B S S J
N A I Z E B U L U N N E I I
C S G M I L A T H P A N N C
```

Words from Words
Treasures

You'll find a lot of treasures in the Bible, words that can make your life richer and happier. And you'll find a lot of words in *treasures*. Follow these rules to solve this puzzle:

1. Each of your words must be at least three letters long.
2. In any one word, you may use a letter only as many times as it appears in *treasures*.
3. No fair adding an *s* to one of your words to make it plural.
4. No foreign words, slang, or words beginning with a capital letter allowed.

We found 48 words. If you find 30 words, you're doing good. If you find 35 words, you're doing great. If you find 40 words or more, you're incredible.

1. _____   7. _____

2. _____   8. _____

3. _____   9. _____

4. _____   10. _____

5. _____   11. _____

6. _____   12. _____

13. _____   31. _____

14. _____   32. _____

15. _____   33. _____

16. _____   34. _____

17. _____   35. _____

18. _____   36. _____

19. _____   37. _____

20. _____   38. _____

21. _____   39. _____

22. _____   40. _____

23. _____   41. _____

24. _____   42. _____

25. _____   43. _____

26. _____   44. _____

27. _____   45. _____

28. _____   46. _____

29. _____   47. _____

30. _____   48. _____

Here's the Middle
Words from the Psalms

Choose a pair of letters from the list below to put in the squares *before* the given letters and another pair to put *after* them. Then you'll have a six-letter word from the Psalms. Each pair of letters will be used once, so cross it off after you use it.

		O	I		
		A	I		
		I	E		
		O	P		
		F	E		
		L	L		
		C	K		

Letter Pairs

AN	PE
ED	PR
EY	SA
SE	SH
LD	TY
LE	VA
NT	WI

Here's the Middle
Bible Animals

Follow the directions from Puzzle 15 to form six-letter names of animals found in the Bible. Each pair of letters will be used once, so cross it off after you use it.

		B	B		
		I	D		
		N	K		
		G	E		
		C	U		
		C	K		
		Z	A		

Letter Pairs

AL	LO
DO	ON
ER	PI
EY	RA
IT	RD
JA	SP
LI	ST

Sneaky Words
New Testament People

Sneaky words hide within sentences, just daring you to find them. In this example, the sneaky word is *scare.*

He doe<u>s care</u> a lot about his son.

Sometimes a sneaky word hides within another word: The word *pit* is found inside the word *sp<u>it</u>e.* Sometimes it takes three or more words to find a sneaky word, and it may even jump over some punctuation. In the sentences below, the sneaky words are all names of people found in the New Testament. See how many you can find and underline.

New Testament People: Agrippa, Andrew, Barnabas, Demas, Dorcas, Herod, Joanna, Justus, Martha, Mary, Nicodemus, Silas

1. There goes Tracey with her odd little purple dog.

2. That new one-stop shopping mart has the best hot dogs in town.

3. Not only did she play the banjo, Ann also accompanied herself with a pedal-operated snare drum.

4. The matador cast his sword before the startled bull and vowed to change his ways.

5. Just behind the barn a baseball diamond was built.

6. Nobody's home except just us four and about a dozen of our best friends.

7. The gardening magazine chose basil as their herb of the month.

8. His mother gave him a rye-bread sandwich.

9. *Do* was the first note in the song and *re* was the second.

10. "Get a grip!" Pa yelled as the piano began to slither down the stairs.

11. He made masses of small wooden figures to use with his model trains.

12. "That Irani code must be broken," said the spy in the gray trench coat.

Scramblie
Bible Plants

These names of Bible plants have been severely scrambled. First, unscramble them and write the answers on the lines provided. Then transfer the letters in circles to the lines below and unscramble them to find another Bible plant.

1. URDOG   __ __ ◯ __ __

2. SORE   ◯ __ __ __

3. NORTH   ◯ __ __ __ __

4. CAMEROSY   __ __ __ __ ◯ __ __ __

5. ATHEW   __ __ __ ◯ __

6. SULTO   __ __ __ __ ◯

7. RACED   __ __ ◯ __ __

__ __ __ __ __ __ __

Words from Words
Beatitudes

You'll find the *Beatitudes,* the "blessed-are-you" statements, in Matthew 5 and Luke 6. How many words can you find in the word *beatitudes*? Here are the rules of the game:

1. Each of your words must be at least three letters long.
2. In any one word, you may use a letter only as many times as it appears in *beatitudes*.
3. No fair adding an *s* to one of your words to make it plural.
4. No foreign words, slang, or words beginning with a capital letter allowed.

We found 87 words. If you find 60 words, you're good. If you find 70 words, you're really good. And if you find 75 words or more, you're really, *really* good!

1. _____   7. _____

2. _____   8. _____

3. _____   9. _____

4. _____   10. _____

5. _____   11. _____

6. _____   12. _____

13. _____

14. _____

15. _____

16. _____

17. _____

18. _____

19. _____

20. _____

21. _____

22. _____

23. _____

24. _____

25. _____

26. _____

27. _____

28. _____

29. _____

30. _____

31. _____

32. _____

33. _____

34. _____

35. _____

36. _____

37. _____

38. _____

39. _____

40. _____

41. _____

42. _____

43. _____

44. _____

45. _____

46. _____

47. _____

48. _____

49. _____

50. _____

51. _____

52. _____

53. _____

54. _____

55. _____

56. _____

57. _____

58. _____

59. _____

60. _____

61. _____

62. _____

63. _____

64. _____

65. _____

66. _____

67. _____

68. _____

69. _____

70. _____

71. _____

72. _____

73. _____

74. _____

75. _____

76. _____

77. _____

78. _____

79. _____

80. _____

81. _____

82. _____

83. _____

84. _____

85. _____

86. _____

87. _____

What's the Verse?
Proverbs 15:13 NIV

Follow the instructions below to cross off words in the puzzle on the opposite page. Then read from left to right, one line at a time, to find out what the Bible verse says.

1. Cross off all words that contain more than two *E*s.

2. Cross off all names of birds.

3. Cross off all words that end with the letter *P*.

4. Cross off all pairs of homonyms (words that sound the same but are spelled differently).

5. Cross off all names of things you might find in the water.

6. Cross off all words that begin with two *L*s.

7. Cross off all words containing a *Q*.

8. Cross off all number words.

A	DOVE	REAP	STEEPLE
CREEPER	FLEE	HEIR	REQUIRE
BOAT	HAPPY	AQUA	HEART
QUICK	FOURTEEN	THOUSAND	SPONGE
MAKES	EQUAL	EAGLE	CLUMP
KEEP	GREENER	THE	FLEA
AIR	MINNOW	LLAMA	ONE
SWALLOW	FACE	PIQUE	SWIFT
TEN	STAMP	SLEEPINESS	CHEERFUL

Sneaky Words
Bible Critters I

Some of these critters are small and some aren't. But they all found places to hide in the sentences below. Sneaky words hide within sentences, just daring you to find them. In this example, the sneaky word is *scare*.

He doe<u>s care</u> a lot about his son.

Sometimes a sneaky word hides within another word: The word *pit* is found inside the word <u>*spit*</u>*e*. Sometimes it takes three or more words to find a sneaky word, and it may even jump over some punctuation. In the sentences below, you'll find names of Bible critters. See how many you can find and underline.

Bible Critters: camel, coney, cow, dove, ewe, heron, hornet, ibex, lamb, leopard, mule, rabbit

1. That mean old crab bit my little toe.

2. Captain Barnes didn't like it when they called his boat a scow.

3. Bozo is her only gerbil, but she has twenty-seven hamsters.

4. The impolite guest came late and stayed late.

5. He threw every single ball over my head.

6. King Leo pardoned the hapless peasants.

7. If you licked my ice cream cone, you're going to be sorry!

8. With a great slurp, he dove into a swimming pool filled with gelatin.

9. Mabel can play the piano, the clarinet, the violin, the horn, etc.

10. If you're looking for a buried bribe, X marks the spot.

11. He likes to slam balls into the basket.

12. The emu leaped about merrily.

Empty Squares
Psalm 16:8

Put the words from the Bible verse below into the empty squares. You will need to make your own word list and no word has been filled in for you.

I have set the Lord always before me. Because He is at my right hand, I will not be shaken. (Psalm 16:8 NIV)

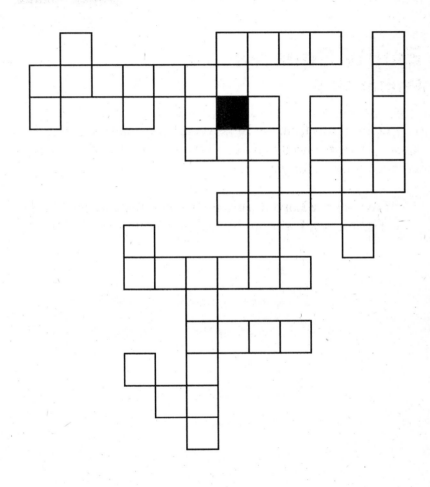

Bible Chain
Places in the Bible

Fill in the links of the chain with the letters of the names described below. The numbers refer to the descriptions and show where each name begins. The last letter of one name will be the first letter of the next. Use the Bible references if you need help.

1. Jesus was crucified outside this city. (Mark 11:27)

2. Moses' father-in-law was a priest here. (Exodus 3:1)

3. Baby Moses floated on this river. (Exodus 2:3)

4. God's people spent a long time here. (Exodus 1:1)

5. The apostle Paul was from this city. (Acts 21:39)

6. All the people of Israel met together here. (Joshua 18:1)

7. Moses saw the burning bush here. (Exodus 3:1–2)

8. Jesus was born in this town. (Luke 2:4)

9. Naomi and her family lived here for a while. (Ruth 1:1–2)

10. Nebuchadnezzar was king of this place. (Daniel 1:1)

11. At the gate of this town, Jesus raised a young man from the dead. (Luke 7:11)

12. God told Jonah to go to this city. (Jonah 1:1–2)

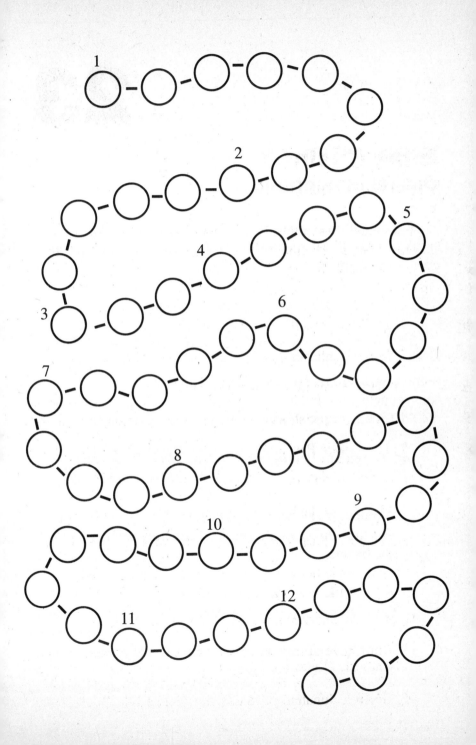

Sneaky Words
Old Testament People I

A group of folks from the Old Testament are serving as sneaky words. Sneaky words hide within sentences, just daring you to find them. In this example, the sneaky word is *scare*.

He does <u>care</u> a lot about his son.

Sometimes a sneaky word hides within another word: The word *pit* is found inside the word *spite*. Sometimes it takes three or more words to find a sneaky word, and it may even jump over some punctuation. In the sentences below, you'll find the names of Old Testament people. See how many you can find and underline.

Old Testament People: Abel, Adam, Ahab, Bathsheba, David, Eve, Ham, Hiram, Issachar, Laban, Naaman, Solomon

1. "Although a shower would be refreshing—not to mention less time-consuming—what I really truly want is a bath," she babbled.

2. He's a little nervous because he has to sing a solo Monday night.

3. Morning brings the birth of a new day, but evening promises rest, sweet rest.

4. Abe Lincoln is one of my heroes.

5. That new store had a video on life in Bible times.

6. If you can hear it hiss, a charcoal fire is still not ready to cook over.

7. "Hi, Rameses, old boy!" said Pharaoh's brother.

8. Fingernail biting is a habit that should be broken.

9. "Hosanna!" a man in the crowd shouted.

10. To a beaver, a dam is a matter of great pride.

11. Meanwhile, back at the lab, another test tube had ex ploded.

12. I have three hamsters, a gerbil, and a guinea pig.

Spelling Test
The Life of King David

Each sentence contains a misspelled word. Find it, circle it, and then write it correctly.

1. David had seven older brothers, but it was David whom Samuel annointed. (1 Samuel 16:13)

2. When Saul was troubled by an evil spirit, David's music gave him releif. (1 Samuel 16:23)

3. David killed Goliath, the Philustine giant, with a sling and a stone. (1 Samuel 17:50)

4. Jonathan was greaved at his father's shameful treatment of David. (1 Samuel 20:34)

5. When old Samuel died, all Isreal mourned for him. (1 Samuel 25:1)

6. When David heard of the deaths of Saul and Jonathan, he sang a great lamment. (2 Samuel 1:17)

7. "How great You are, O Sovreign Lord!" prayed David. (2 Samuel 7:22)

8. For the most part, David was a righteous king, and God blessed him. (2 Samuel 23:3–5)

9. When David was old, he said his son Solomon should rain after him. (1 Kings 1:35)

10. Solomon made an allience with Pharaoh and married his daughter. (1 Kings 3:1)

11. Solomon asked God for a discerning heart to govern God's people and distingwish between right and wrong. (1 Kings 3:9)

12. When Solomon built a temple for the Lord, he used wood from the ceders of Lebanon. (1 Kings 5:6)

Word Search
The Journey

You'll find the words for this puzzle in Exodus 13–40, which tells how Moses led God's people out of Egypt and through the wilderness. How many words can you find? Look for them up or down, from side to side, or diagonally. Circle each word as you find it and mark it off the list.

ANGEL
ARK
CHARIOTS
CLOUD
COMMANDMENTS
COVENANT
DANCING
DESERT
FIRE
GLORY
GOLDEN CALF
GROUND
GRUMBLING
JETHRO

JOSHUA
LIGHTNING
MANNA
MIRIAM
PILLAR
QUAIL
RED SEA
SINAI
SMOKE
SONG
TABERNACLE
TABLETS
TENT
WATER

```
G T J G C H A R I O T S M O D
V O A O L I I D K R A A R A U
E G L B S O X A E Y N H N C D
L N T D L H R W Q N T C O U C
C I E E E U Y A E I M O J O
A N N I R N T A J N M L B X V
N T T Y L I C S G A C F X H E
R H P D F O F A N P Q A D F N
E G K M I M D D L G I U U Z A
B I R A A E M A H F R L A K N
A L N I S E E R M E A O L I T
T I R E N S E U L V K N U A L
S I R T D T Z V H U L O G N R
M T S E A H N C G N O S M E D
C B R W G R U M B L I N G S L
```

Sneaky Words
Bible Books II

Sneaky words hide within sentences, just daring you to find them. In this example, the sneaky word is *scare*.

He doe<u>s care</u> a lot about his son.

Sometimes a sneaky word hides within another word: The word *pit* is found inside the word *spite*. Sometimes it takes three or more words to find a sneaky word, and it may even jump over some punctuation. In the sentences below, the sneaky words are all names of books of the Bible. See how many you can find and underline.

Bible Books: Esther, Hebrews, James, Judges, Kings, Micah, Peter, Philemon, Romans, Thessalonians, Titus

1. They say Judge Smith is tough on crooks.

2. I hope termites haven't taken over the house.

3. Emmet Kelly was a special sort of comic, a hobo comic.

4. If that shy boy asks you to the prom, answer him gently.

5. Grandma's strawberry jam established her as the best cook in town.

6. Mom said to Pop, "Hi! Lemonade is in the refrigerator."

7. Though I like to have my hair done at Ianthe's salon, Ian's is cheaper.

8. He brews the best root beer in the country.

9. Although our church service is fairly short, it used to seem long to me when I was little.

10. If I were king, school would be completely voluntary.

11. While the female robin stayed in the nest, her mate chased other birds away.

Empty Squares
Psalm 148:13

Put the words from the Bible verse below into the empty squares. To help you, we've listed the words according to the number of letters in each. And we've placed one word to get you started.

Let them praise the name of the Lord, for His name alone is exalted; His splendor is above the earth and the heavens. (Psalm 148:13 NIV)

2-letter words
is
is
of

3-letter words
and
for
His
His
let
the
the
the
the

4-letter words
Lord
name
name
them

5-letter words
above
alone
earth

6-letter words
praise

7-letter words
exalted
heavens

8-letter words
splendor

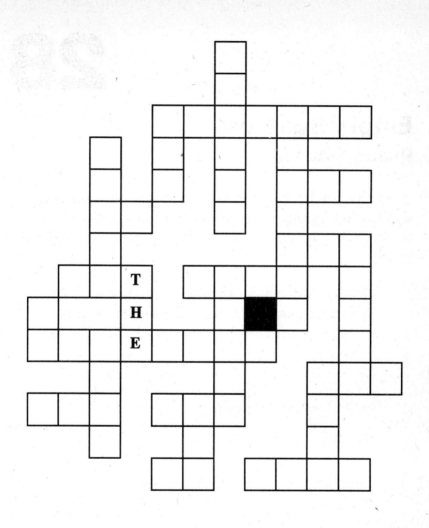

Scramblie
Names for God

Words that are names for God have been severely scrambled. First, unscramble them and write the answers on the lines provided. Then transfer the letters in circles to the lines below and unscramble them to find another name for God.

1. CORK __ ◯ __ __

2. GOLDTHORNS __ ◯ __ __ __ __ __ __ __ __

3. DEJUG __ __ __ __◯

4. DELISH ◯ __ __ __ __ __

5. GUFREE __ __ ◯ __ __ __

6. RIVERDEEL __ __ __ __ __ __ __ __◯

7. PHREEL __ __ __ __ __ ◯

8. ASTONIVAL ◯ __ __ __ __ __ __ __ __

__ __ __ __ __ __ __

Words from Words
Prophets

The Bible is full of prophets. And the word *prophets* is full of many other words. How many words can you find? Here are the rules:

1. Each word must be at least three letters long.
2. In any one word, you may use a letter only as many times as it appears in the word *prophets.*
3. No fair adding an *s* to one of your words to make it plural.
4. No foreign words, slang, or words beginning with a capital letter allowed.

We found 55 words. If you find 30 words, that's good. If you find 40 words, that's great. And if you find 45 words or more, that's absolutely super.

1. _____   6. _____

2. _____   7. _____

3. _____   8. _____

4. _____   9. _____

5. _____   10. _____

11. _____   28. _____

12. _____   29. _____

13. _____   30. _____

14. _____   31. _____

15. _____   32. _____

16. _____   33. _____

17. _____   34. _____

18. _____   35. _____

19. _____   36. _____

20. _____   37. _____

21. _____   38. _____

22. _____   39. _____

23. _____   40. _____

24. _____   41. _____

25. _____   42. _____

26. _____   43. _____

27. _____   44. _____

45. _____

46. _____

47. _____

48. _____

49. _____

50. _____

51. _____

52. _____

53. _____

54. _____

55. _____

Word Search
Esther

You'll find the words for this puzzle in the Book of Esther. How many words can you find? Look for them up or down, from side to side, or diagonally. Circle each word as you find it and mark it off the list.

BANQUET
DECREE
ESTHER
GALLOWS
GATE
GLADNESS
HAMAN
HATHACH
HORSE
JOY
MORDECAI
PALACE
PERSIA

PETITION
PLUNDER
POWER
PURIM
RING
SACKCLOTH
SCEPTER
SORROW
SUSA
TERESH
VASHTI
XERXES
ZERESH

```
S R N P E T I T I O N H E F
H C E A K K E T A G O C E P
T C E H M Y V F J R A E L S
S E A P T A S D S L R U W J
P A U H T S H E A C N O S S
D E C Q T E E P E D L S O E
R H R K N A R D E L E R I M
S E T S C A H R A N R T I Z
U I W E I L B G D O H R C E
S J W O R A O A W S U E H R
A M K Z P E L T A P P N I E
I R Z H H G S V H O H L Y S
Q S E X R E X H S R J H O H
M O R D E C A I R I N G J T
```

What's the Verse?
Proverbs 12:19 NIV

Follow the instructions below to cross off words in the puzzle on the opposite page. Then read from left to right, one line at a time, to find out what the Bible verse says.

1. Cross off all words of three letters and less.

2. Cross off all words containing a *K*.

3. Cross off all words that rhyme with *light*.

4. Cross off all things that might be found in the sky.

5. Cross off all words that are also words when read backwards.

6. Cross off all names of animals.

7. Cross off all words beginning with *I*.

8. Cross off all words with more than one *P*.

NIGHT	WORK	REED	OF
MOUSE	FLIGHT	BUG	IMPRESS
TRUTHFUL	MOON	BEAR	PUMPKIN
INTO	PERHAPS	MEEKNESS	STUN
TO	IRRITATE	CLOUD	WHALE
BUTTERFLY	LIPS	PROPHET	KNOW
POTS	LION	SPITE	ENDURE
PEPPER	PANS	ITALY	A
FOREVER	MY	PAPYRUS	BITE

Scramblie
Jesus' Friends

The names of Jesus' friends have been severely scrambled. First, unscramble them and write the answers on the lines provided. Then transfer the letters in circles to the lines below and unscramble them to find yet another of Jesus' friends.

1. MINSO   __ __ O __ __

2. HATOMS   O __ __ __ __ __

3. ARMY   __ O __ __

4. HIPPLI   __ O __ __ __ __

5. AZULARS   __ O __ __ __ __ __

6. TEREP   __ __ __ __ O

__ __ __ __ __ __

Words from Words
Sennacherib

Sennacherib was a king of Assyria in Old Testament times. God sent an angel to win a mighty victory over him. The name *Sennacherib* is so full of words that it's time to change the rules. For this puzzle, here are the new rules:

1. Each of your words must be at least four letters long. (No three-letter words allowed.)
2. In any one word, you may use a letter only as many times as it appears in *Sennacherib*.
3. No fair adding an *s* to one of your words to make it plural.
4. No foreign words, slang, or words beginning with a capital letter allowed.

We found 100 words. If you find 70 words, smile. If you find 80, grin. And if you find 85 words or more, do handsprings.

1. _____   7. _____

2. _____   8. _____

3. _____   9. _____

4. _____   10. _____

5. _____   11. _____

6. _____   12. _____

13. _____   35. _____

14. _____   36. _____

15. _____   37. _____

16. _____   38. _____

17. _____   39. _____

18. _____   40. _____

19. _____   41. _____

20. _____   42. _____

21. _____   43. _____

22. _____   44. _____

23. _____   45. _____

24. _____   46. _____

25. _____   47. _____

26. _____   48. _____

27. _____   49. _____

28. _____   50. _____

29. _____   51. _____

30. _____   52. _____

31. _____   53. _____

32. _____   54. _____

33. _____   55. _____

34. _____   56. _____

57. _____

58. _____

59. _____

60. _____

61. _____

62. _____

63. _____

64. _____

65. _____

66. _____

67. _____

68. _____

69. _____

70. _____

71. _____

72. _____

73. _____

74. _____

75. _____

76. _____

77. _____

78. _____

79. _____

80. _____

81. _____

82. _____

83. _____

84. _____

85. _____

86. _____

87. _____

88. _____

89. _____

90. _____

91. _____

92. _____

93. _____

94. _____

95. _____

96. _____

97. _____

98. _____

99. _____

100. _____

Sneaky Words
Bible Plants

See how many Bible plants you can unearth in the sneaky - word sentences below. Sneaky words hide within sentences, just daring you to find them. In this example, the sneaky word is *scare*.

He doe<u>s care</u> a lot about his son.

Sometimes a sneaky word hides within another word: The word *pit* is found inside the word *s<u>pit</u>e*. Sometimes it takes three or more words to find a sneaky word, and it may even jump over some punctuation. In the sentences below, the sneaky words are all names of plants found in the Bible. See how many you can find and underline.

Bible Plants: apple, cedar, fig, gourd, grape, oak, olive, palm, plane, reed, rose, thorn

1. No matter how hard I try, I can't figure out what they want.

2. Do Meg, Beth, Amy, and Jo live on this street?

3. Allegra peeked through the window and clapped her hands in delight.

4. "Won't you be a good boy and take a nap?" pleaded the weary mother.

5. "I have a ring with a ruby in it and one with an opal," Monica boasted.

6. The lion paced around the cage as if longing for his home in the wild.

7. The author never showed up for the book-signing because she couldn't find a parking place.

8. Never offer bubble gum to a kid with braces.

9. Would you please stop ringing our doorbell!

10. We all agreed that Christmas was our favorite holiday.

11. Burros eat less than horses and can be quite loveable.

12. "It's a great plan," Elmer said, "but it won't work."

Empty Squares
Psalm 9:9

Put the words from the Bible verse below into the empty squares. For an extra challenge, this time you have to make your own word list and no word has been filled in for you.

**The Lord is a refuge for the oppressed,
a stronghold in times of trouble. (Psalm 9:9 NIV)**

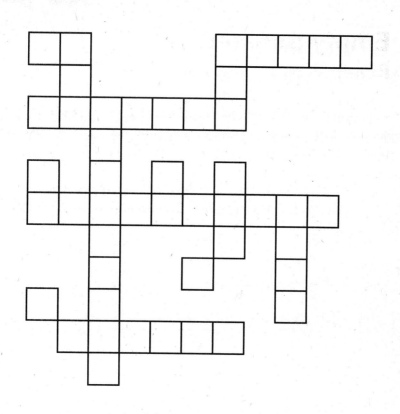

Scramblie
Words from Psalm 84

Words from Psalm 84 have been severely scrambled. First, unscramble them and write the answers on the lines provided. Then transfer the letters in circles to the lines below and unscramble them to find another word from Psalm 84.

1. CLEAP   __ __ __ __ ◯

2. TARAL   __ __ __ __ ◯

3. VELLOY   __ __ __ __ __ ◯

4. STIFAN   __ __ __ ◯ __ __

5. AWLOWLS   __ __ ◯ __ __ __ __

6. SEBSLED   __ __ __ ◯ __ __ __

__ __ __ __ __ __

Words from Words
Pharisees

Some of those Pharisees in the Bible spouted words like geysers. The word *Pharisees* holds a good number of words too. How many can you find? A few rules:

1. Each of your words must be at least three letters long.
2. In any one word, you may use a letter only as many times at it appears in *Pharisees*.
3. No fair adding an *s* to one of your words to make it plural.
4. No foreign words, slang, or words beginning with a capital letter allowed.

We found 72 words. If you find 50 words, you've done fine. Finding 55 is fabulous, and finding 60 words or more is spectacular.

1. _____

2. _____

3. _____

4. _____

5. _____

6. _____

7. _____

8. _____

9. _____

10. _____

11. _____

12. _____

13. _____   34. _____

14. _____   35. _____

15. _____   36. _____

16. _____   37. _____

17. _____   38. _____

18. _____   39. _____

19. _____   40. _____

20. _____   41. _____

21. _____   42. _____

22. _____   43. _____

23. _____   44. _____

24. _____   45. _____

25. _____   46. _____

26. _____   47. _____

27. _____   48. _____

28. _____   49. _____

29. _____   50. _____

30. _____   51. _____

31. _____   52. _____

32. _____   53. _____

33. _____   54. _____

55. _____

56. _____

57. _____

58. _____

59. _____

60. _____

61. _____

62. _____

63. _____

64. _____

65. _____

66. _____

67. _____

68. _____

69. _____

70. _____

71. _____

72. _____

Sneaky Words
Old Testament People II

You'll find the names of still more Old Testament people hiding in the sneaky-word sentences below. Sneaky words hide within sentences, just daring you to find them. In this example, the sneaky word is *scare*.

He doe<u>s care</u> a lot about his son.

Sometimes a sneaky word hides within another word: The word *pit* is found inside the word *spite*. Sometimes it takes three or more words to find a sneaky word, and it may even jump over some punctuation. In the sentences below, the sneaky words are all names of Old Testament people. See how many you can find and underline.

Old Testament People: Abednego, Boaz, Caleb, Dinah, Esau, Gideon, Goliath, Haman, Noah, Obed, Rachel, Tamar

1. He finds "no" a hard word to say sometimes.

2. My Aunt Florence is not only eccentric, she's a unique person.

3. "This house is ready to explode with bric-a-brac," he laughed.

4. The Ice Age was a frigid eon.

5. I find Bobo a zany sort of clown.

6. Most parents prefer obedient children.

7. Most people in Mongolia think lollipops an unnecessary import.

8. Percale bedclothes are comfortable and easy to care for.

9. Ham and eggs make a dandy breakfast.

10. "I'll give you four chairs for a bed," negotiated the furniture trader.

11. The crowd watching the parade made such a din, a horse turned around and ran the other way.

12. In an orange tam, a red coat, and yellow boots, she was a colorful sight.

Bible Chain
Old Testament People

Fill in the links of this chain with the letters of the names described below. The numbers refer to the descriptions and show where each name begins. The last letter of one name will be the first letter of the next. Use the Bible references if you need help.

1. He was the first man. (Genesis 2:20)

2. She was Moses' and Aaron's sister. (Exodus 15:20)

3. He was one of the three men in the fiery furnace. (Daniel 3:19-20)

4. She was Samuel's mother. (1 Samuel 1:20)

5. She was Ishmael's mother. (Genesis 16:15)

6. He kept his brothers from killing Joseph. (Genesis 37:21–22)

7. She was Ruth's mother-in-law. (Ruth 1:6)

8. He was born when Abraham and Sarah were quite old. (Genesis 21:3)

9. He worked as a spy in Canaan. (Numbers 13:6)

10. She was one of David's wives. (2 Samuel 12:24)

11. She helped David and his soldiers. (1 Samuel 25:32)

12. He was Jacob's uncle. (Genesis 29:10)

Scramblie
Words from the Peaceful Kingdom

The peaceful kingdom is described in Isaiah 11:6–9. Words from this Bible reference have been severely scrambled. First, unscramble them and write the answers on the lines provided. Then transfer the letters in circles to the lines below and unscramble them to find another word from Isaiah 11:6–9.

1. GUYON   __ __ O __ __

2. TANFIN   __ O __ __ __ __

3. BALM   __ __ O __

4. TAGO   __ __ __ O

5. ONLI   __ __ __ O

6. FLOW   __ O __ __

7. WARTS   __ __ __ O __

8. DILCH   __ __ O __ __

__ __ __ __ __ __ __ __

Words from Words
Bartholomew

We don't hear as many stories about Bartholomew as about some of Jesus' other disciples. But he certainly has a name full of words. Rules are as follows:

1. Each of your words must be at least four letters long. (No three-letter words allowed.)
2. In any one word, you may use a letter only as many times as it appears in *Bartholomew.*
3. No fair adding an *s* to one of your words to make it plural.
4. No foreign words, slang, or words beginning with a capital letter allowed.

We found 133 words. If you can find 85 words, you've done a nice job. Finding 95 is marvelous. If you can find 105 words or more—WOW!

1. _____   6. _____

2. _____   7. _____

3. _____   8. _____

4. _____   9. _____

5. _____   10. _____

11. _____

12. _____

13. _____

14. _____

15. _____

16. _____

17. _____

18. _____

19. _____

20. _____

21. _____

22. _____

23. _____

24. _____

25. _____

26. _____

27. _____

28. _____

29. _____

30. _____

31. _____

32. _____

33. _____

34. _____

35. _____

36. _____

37. _____

38. _____

39. _____

40. _____

41. _____

42. _____

43. _____

44. _____

45. _____

46. _____

47. _____

48. _____

49. _____

50. _____

51. _____

52. _____

53. _____

54. _____

55. _____

56. _____

57. _____

58. _____

59. _____

60. _____

61. _____

62. _____

63. _____

64. _____

65. _____

66. _____

67. _____

68. _____

69. _____

70. _____

71. _____

72. _____

73. _____

74. _____

75. _____

76. _____

77. _____

78. _____

79. _____

80. _____

81. _____

82. _____

83. _____

84. _____

85. _____

86. _____

87. _____

88. _____

89. _____

90. _____

91. _____

92. _____

93. _____

94. _____

95. _____

96. _____

97. _____

98. _____

99. _____

100. _____

101. _____

102. _____

103. _____

104. _____

105. _____

106. _____

107. _____

108. _____

109. _____

110. _____

111. _____

112. _____

113. _____

114. _____

115. _____

116. _____

117. _____

118. _____

119. _____

120. _____

121. _____

122. _____

123. _____

124. _____

125. _____

126. _____

127. _____

128. _____

129. _____

130. _____

131. _____

132. _____

133. _____

Word Search
Elijah

You'll find the words for this puzzle in 1 Kings 17–2 Kings 2, the story of the prophet Elijah. How many words can you find? Look for them up or down, from side to side, or diagonally. Circle each word as you find it and mark it off the list.

AHAB	JERICHO
BAAL	JEZEBEL
BREAD	JORDAN
BROOK	KERITH
BROOM TREE	MEAT
CARMEL	OBADIAH
CHARIOT	PORTION
CHILD	PROPHETS
CLOAK	RAVENS
EARTHQUAKE	SACRIFICE
ELIJAH	TISHBITE
ELISHA	WHIRLWIND
FIRE	WHISPER
HOREB	WIDOW
HORSES	ZAREPHATH

```
J R N B Y S R A L L I P S S O
E N A I L L J I O F D N L N L
R I S T A U I M G E I L S O C
U B T P L H E L D S U G R R U
S A E G O A C I A B N D L V R
A M L Y R M C B P I R Z B K T
L A B D L A E C W U M Q M L A
E R A Z T C O G H E R N F E I
M U T I U E G A R E Z P R K N
Y H O B L O L W U A R N L A Q
X N I P L Y E E I U N U O E Y
Z T M D N O M O L O S A B R R
S E J K N N O S M I R C T I B
T R R L A M P S T A N D F E M
G A C O U R T Y A R D Q F U S
```

44

Sneaky Words
Bible Critters II

Twelve more critters dare you to find them in the sneaky-word sentences below. Sneaky words hide within sentences, just daring you to find them. In this example, the sneaky word is *scare*.

He doe<u>s care</u> a lot about his son.

Sometimes a sneaky word hides within another word: The word *pit* is found inside the word *s<u>pit</u>e*. Sometimes it takes three or more words to find a sneaky word, and it may even jump over some punctuation. In the sentences below, the sneaky words are all critters found in the Bible. See how many you can find and underline.

Bible Critters: antelope, bear, cobra, eagle, flies, horse, lion, osprey, quail, rooster, snake, stork

1. Well, I'll be a roadrunner's uncle!

2. "Don't you dare pick my pocket," said the kangaroo sternly.

3. I prefer my corn on the cob rather than cut into a dish.

4. Those sweet little burros prey on absolutely no other creature.

5. Liverwurst or kale—he'll eat anything.

6. We all abhor senseless violence.

7. Belinda the Wonder Beagle sang patriotic songs while waving a flag with her tail.

8. If you'll paint the walls aqua, I'll stick up some fish pictures.

9. The story tells how a peasant eloped with a king.

10. I must have pulled thousands of dandelions today.

11. A dishonest mouth is full of lies.

12. On such a cold day, his naked foot was turning blue.

Answers

Puzzle 1: Bible People Pyramid—Bible Men

Dan, Paul, Jacob, Joseph, Lazarus, Abednego, Nicodemus, Belshazzar, Bartholomew

Puzzle 2: Word Search—The Flood

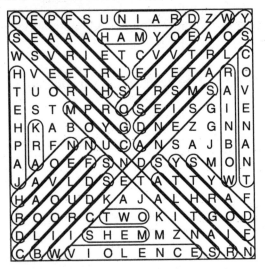

Puzzle 3: Sneaky Words—Bible Places

1. Let the Welsh cor<u>gi lead</u> the dog parade.
2. Those mean kids knocked over Sal<u>ly's trash</u> can.
3. If that's an or<u>der, be</u> sure to obey it.
4. When he saw what the sergeant had done, the ma<u>jor</u> <u>dan</u>ced with fury and his face turned purple.
5. <u>She bronz</u>ed Johnny's little shoes so she could keep them forever.
6. A hole is home to a fox, a <u>pit home</u> to a viper.
7. "Aren't you ever going to <u>go?" she n</u>agged her frazzled husband.
8. We left the s<u>hore by</u> another road.
9. It was so hot there in the desert, his <u>car mel</u>ted into a puddle of plastic.
10. My mother is the best ba<u>ker, I think</u>.
11. Although he's a fine tenor, for <u>Sam arias</u> are difficult to sing.
12. "You're absolutely right, my dear," he <u>nodded</u>.

Puzzle 4: Empty Squares—Psalm 47:1–2

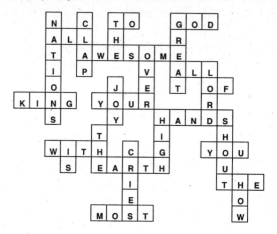

Puzzle 5: Words from Words—Matthew

ate, awe, eat, ham, hat, hate, heat, hem, hew, mat, mate, math, matte, meat, met, mew, tam, tame, tat, tea, team, that, thaw, the, them, wet, what, wheat, whet

Puzzle 6: Bible People Pyramid—Bible Women

Eve, Mary, Rhoda, Hannah, Deborah, Zipporah, Bathsheba

Puzzle 7: Scramblie—Psalm 23

1. comfort; 2. table; 3. enemies; 4. shadow; 5. green; 6. waters; 7. house; 8. shepherd   **GOODNESS**

Puzzle 8: What's the Verse?—Proverbs 26:20

Without gossip a quarrel dies down.

Puzzle 9: Fill 'Em Up—Bible Things

Leah, Lot, Lystra, Lion
Anna, Adam, Antioch, Ant
Mary, Moses, Moriah, Moth
Priscilla, Paul, Persia, Pig

Puzzle 10: Fill 'Em Up—Things Said in Church

Wonderful; Welcoming; "What a friend we have in Jesus";
"We Three Kings"
Almighty; Alive; "Abide with me"; "Away in a Manger"
Strong; Sinless; "Savior, again to Your dear name we raise";
"Silent Night"
High; Holy; "Holy, holy, holy"; "Hark! The Herald Angels Sing"

Puzzle 11: Words from Words—Jeremiah

aim, air, are, arm, ear, era, hair, ham, hare, harem, harm, hear, hem,
her, here, him, hire, ire, jam, jar, jeer, mar, mare, mere, mire, ram,
ream, rim

Puzzle 12: Sneaky Words—Bible Books I

1. If you can't find your Bible, <u>Gene's is</u> over there.
2. I can't <u>act, so</u> I'm painting scenery for the school play.
3. Our pastor says that perh<u>aps alms</u>-giving might be part of our
   stewardship program.
4. To a real grammar <u>pro, verbs</u> are a snap.
5. Sam did a good <u>job</u>, but he hurt his foot in the process.
6. Mom says it's best always to tell the <u>truth</u>.
7. In India, a <u>raj on a h</u>orse is a splendid sight.
8. Look at <u>Rev. Elati on</u> his motorcycle!
9. The <u>mat the w</u>ind carried away is under the lilac bush.
10. A whale's tail is called a <u>fluke</u>.
11. We don't like this cleanser because it can <u>mar k</u>itchen counters.

Puzzle 13: Word Search—Joseph and His Brothers

Puzzle 14: Words from Words—Treasures

are, art, assert, asset, assure, aster, ate, ear, ease, east, eat, era, erase,
rare, rat, rate, rear, reassure, reset, rest, rue, ruse, rust, rut, sat, sate,
sea, sear, seat, see, seer, sere, set, star, stare, steer, sue, sure, tar, tare,
tea, tear, tease, teaser, tress, true, tsar, use

Puzzle 15: Here's the Middle—Words from the Psalms

anoint, praise, shield, people, safety, valley, wicked

Puzzle 16: Here's the Middle—Bible Animals

rabbit, spider, donkey, pigeon, locust, jackal, lizard

Puzzle 17: Sneaky Words—New Testament People

1. There goes Tracey with <u>her od</u>d little purple dog.
2. That new one-stop shopping <u>mart ha</u>s the best hot dogs in town.
3. Not only did she play the ban<u>jo, Ann a</u>lso accompanied herself
   with a pedal-operated snare drum.
4. The mata<u>dor cast</u> his sword before the startled bull and vowed to
   change his ways.
5. Just behind the <u>barn a base</u>ball diamond was built.
6. Nobody's home except <u>just us</u> four and about a dozen of our best
   friends.
7. The gardening magazine chose ba<u>sil as</u> their herb of the month.
8. His mother gave hi<u>m a rye</u>-bread sandwich.
9. *Do* was the first note in the song <u>and *re* w</u>as the second.
10. "Get <u>a grip!" Pa</u> yelled as the piano began to slither down the
    stairs.
11. He ma<u>de mass</u>es of small wooden figures to use with his model
    trains.
12. "That Ira<u>ni code must</u> be broken," said the spy in the gray trench
    coat.

Puzzle 18: Scramblie—Bible Plants

1. gourd; 2. rose; 3. thorn; 4. sycamore; 5. wheat; 6. lotus; 7. cedar
MUSTARD

Puzzle 19: Words from Words—Beatitudes

abet, abide, aid, aide, aside, astute, ate, bad, bait, baste, bat, batted, beast, beat, bee, beside, best, bet, bide, bit, bite, bud, bust, but, butt, butte, butted, dab, date, debate, debt, debut, detest, die, diet, dub, due, duet, dust, ease, eased, east, edit, estate, etude, idea, sad, said, sat, sate, sated, sea, see, seed, set, side, sit, site, stab, staid, state, stated, steed, stub, stud, sub, sue, sued, suet, suit, suite, suited, tab, tad, taste, tat, tea, tease, teased, tee, test, tide, tie, tied, tub, tuba, tube

Puzzle 20: What's the Verse—Proverbs 15:13

A happy heart makes the face cheerful.

Puzzle 21: Sneaky Words—Bible Critters I

1. That mean old c<u>rab bit</u> my little toe.
2. Captain Barnes didn't like it when they called his boat a s<u>cow</u>.
3. Bozo is <u>her on</u>ly gerbil, but she has twenty-seven hamsters.
4. The impolite guest <u>came l</u>ate and stayed late.
5. He th<u>rew e</u>very single ball over my head.
6. King <u>Leo pard</u>oned the hapless peasants.
7. If you licked my ice cream <u>cone, y</u>ou're going to be sorry!
8. With a great slurp, he <u>dove</u> into a swimming pool filled with gelatin.
9. Mabel can play the piano, the clarinet, the violin, the <u>horn, et</u>c.
10. If you're looking for a buried br<u>ibe, X</u> marks the spot.
11. He likes to s<u>lam b</u>alls into the basket.
12. The e<u>mu l</u>eaped about merrily.

Puzzle 22: Empty Squares—Psalm 16:8

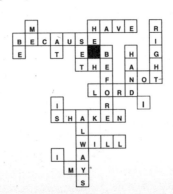

Puzzle 23: Bible Chain—Places in the Bible

1. Jerusalem; 2. Midian; 3. Nile; 4. Egypt; 5. Tarsus; 6. Shiloh;
7. Horeb; 8. Bethlehem; 9. Moab; 10. Babylon; 11. Nain; 12. Nineveh

Puzzle 24: Sneaky Words—Old Testament People I

1. "Although a shower would be refreshing--not to mention less time-consuming--what I really truly want is a <u>bath," she ba</u>bbled.
2. He's a little nervous because he has to sing a <u>solo Mon</u>day night.
3. Morning brings the birth of a new day, but <u>even</u>ing promises rest, sweet rest.
4. <u>Abe L</u>incoln is one of my heroes.
5. That new store ha<u>d a vide</u>o on life in Bible times.
6. If you can hear it h<u>iss, a char</u>coal fire is still not ready to cook over.
7. "<u>Hi, Ram</u>eses, old boy!" said Pharaoh's brother.
8. Fingernail biting is <u>a habit</u> that should be broken.
9. "Hosan<u>na!" a man</u> in the crowd shouted.
10. To a beaver, <u>a dam</u> is a matter of great pride.
11. Meanwhile, back at the <u>lab, ano</u>ther test tube had exploded.
12. I have three <u>ham</u>sters, a gerbil, and a guinea pig.

Puzzle 25: Spelling Test—The Life of King David

1. annointed/anointed
2. releif/relief
3. Philustine/Philistine
4. greaved/grieved
5. Isreal/Israel
6. lamment/lament
7. Sovreign/Sovereign
8. rightous/righteous
9. rain/reign
10. allience/alliance
11. distingwish/distinguish
12. ceders/cedars

Puzzle 26: Word Search—The Journey

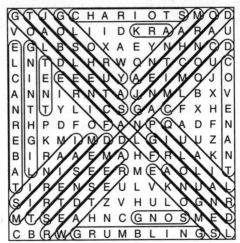

Puzzle 27: Sneaky Words—Bible Books II

1. They say <u>Judge S</u>mith is tough on crooks.
2. I hope <u>termites</u> haven't taken over the house.
3. Emmet Kelly was a special sort of co<u>mic, a h</u>obo comic.
4. If that shy boy asks you to the p<u>rom, ans</u>wer him gently.
5. Grandma's strawberry <u>jam es</u>tablished her as the best cook in town.
6. Mom said to Po<u>p, "Hi! Lemon</u>ade is in the refrigerator."
7. Though I like to have my hair done at Ia<u>nthe's salon, Ian's</u> is cheaper.
8. <u>He brews</u> the best root beer in the country.
9. Although our church service is fairly shor<u>t, it us</u>ed to seem long to me when I was little.
10. If I were <u>king, s</u>chool would be completely voluntary.
11. While the female robin stayed in the n<u>est, her</u> mate chased other birds away.

Puzzle 28: Empty Squares—Psalm 148:13

Puzzle 29: Scramblie—Names for God

1. rock; 2. stronghold; 3. judge; 4. shield; 5. refuge; 6. deliverer;
7. helper; 8. salvation
FORTRESS

Puzzle 30: Words from Words—Prophets

hero, hoe, hop, hope, hopper, horse, hose, host, opt, ore, pep, pert,
pest, pet, poet, pop, pope, pore, port, pose, posh, post, poster, prep,
pro, prop, prose, rep, rest, rope, rose, rot, rote, set, shoe, shop,
shopper, shore, short, shot, sop, sore, spore, sport, spot, step, stop,
stopper, store, strep, the, those, toe, top, tore

Puzzle 31: Word Search—Esther

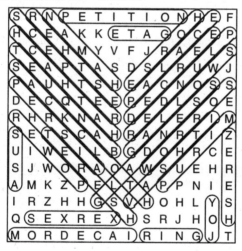

Puzzle 32: What's the Verse?—Proverbs 12:19

Truthful lips endure forever.

Puzzle 33: Scramblie—Jesus' Friends

1. Simon; 2. Thomas; 3. Mary; 4. Philip; 5. Lazarus; 6. Peter
MARTHA

Puzzle 34: Words from Words—Sennacherib

ache, anise, arch, arise, arisen, ashen, bane, banner, banns, bare, barn, base, bash, beach, bean, bear, beech, been, beer, bench, bier, birch, brace, brain, bran, branch, brash, breach, cabin, cane, canine, canner, care, case, cease, chain, chair, chaise, char, chase, cheer, chin, china, crab, crane, crash, crease, crib, cries, earn, ease, enhance, hair, hare, hear, hearse, henna, herb, hire, inane, inch, inner, insane, near, nice, niche, niece, nine, rabies, race, rain, ranch, rash, reach, rein, rice, rich, rinse, rise, sane, scab, scan, scar, scare, scene, sear, search, seen, seer, sere, share, shear, sheen, sheer, shine, shire, shrine, since, sincere, sinner

Puzzle 35: Sneaky Words—Bible Plants

1. No matter how hard I try, I can't <u>figu</u>re out what they want.
2. Do Meg, Beth, Amy, and J<u>o live</u> on this street?
3. Alle<u>gra pe</u>eked through the window and clapped her hands in delight.
4. "Won't you be a good boy and take a n<u>ap?" ple</u>aded the weary mother.
5. "I have a ring with a ruby in it and one with an o<u>pal," M</u>onica boasted.
6. The lion pa<u>ced ar</u>ound the cage as if longing for his home in the wild.
7. The au<u>thor n</u>ever showed up for the book-signing because she couldn't find a parking place.
8. Never offer bubble gum t<u>o a k</u>id with braces.
9. Would you please stop ringing<u> our d</u>oorbell!
10. We all a<u>greed</u> that Christmas was our favorite holiday.
11. Bur<u>ros e</u>at less than horses and can be quite loveable.
12. "It's a great <u>plan," E</u>lmer said, "but it won't work.

Puzzle 36: Empty Squares—Psalm 9:9

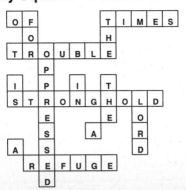

Puzzle 37: Scramblie—Words from Psalm 84
1. place; 2. altar; 3. lovely; 4. faints; 5. swallow; 6. blessed
YEARNS

Puzzle 38: Words from Words—Pharisees
air, ape, are, arise, ash, asp, aspire, ear, ease, hair, hare, harp, harpies, heap, hearse, her, here, hire, his, hiss, ire, pair, par, pare, pass, pea, pear, peer, phase, phrase, pie, pier, praise, press, pries, raise, rap, rash, rasp, reap, rip, ripe, rise, sap, sash, sea, sear, see, seep, seer, seraph, sere, shape, share, sharp, she, shear, sheep, sheer, ship, shire, sip, sir, sire, sis, spa, spar, spare, spear, spies, spire, spree

Puzzle 39: Sneaky Words—Old Testament People II
1. He finds "no" a hard word to say sometimes.
2. My Aunt Florence is not only eccentric, she's a unique person.
3. This house is ready to explode with bric-a-brac," he laughed.
4. The Ice Age was a frigid eon.
5. I find Bobo a zany sort of clown.
6. Most parents prefer obedient children.
7. Most people in Mongolia think lollipops an unnecessary import.
8. Percale bedclothes are comfortable and easy to care for.
9. Ham and eggs make a dandy breakfast.
10. "I'll give you four chairs for a bed," negotiated the furniture trader.
11. The crowd watching the parade made such a din, a horse turned around and ran the other way.
12. In an orange tam, a red coat, and yellow boots, she was a colorful sight.

Puzzle 40: Bible Chain—Old Testament People
1. Adam; 2. Miriam; 3. Meshach; 4. Hannah; 5. Hagar; 6. Reuben;
7. Naomi; 8. Isaac; 9. Caleb; 10. Bathsheba; 11. Abigail; 12. Laban

Puzzle 41: Scramblie—Isaiah 11:6–9
1. young; 2. infant; 3. lamb; 4. goat; 5. lion; 6. wolf; 7. straw; 8. child
MOUNTAIN

Puzzle 42: Words from Words—Bartholomew

able, alter, alto, amber, amble, bale, bare, bath, bathe, bawl, bear, beat, belt, berth, blame, blare, bleat, bloat, bloom, blow, blower, boar, boat, bolt, boom, boot, booth, bore, both, bother, bower, bowl, brat, brew, broom, broth, brow, earth, hale, halo, halt, halter, hare, harm, hart, hate, heal, hear, heart, heat, herb, herbal, hero, hobo, home, hoot, hotel, labor, lamb, lame, late, later, lathe, loam, loathe, lobe, loom, loot, lore, lower, male, malt, marble, mare, mart, math, meal, meat, melt, moat, molar, mole, molt, moor, moot, more, mote, motel, moth, mother, oath, other, owlet, ramble, real, realm, ream, roam, role, room, root, table, tale, tame, tamer, tare, teal, team, tear, thaw, threw, throb, throw, tomb, tome, tore, towel, tower, warble, warm, wart, wealth, wear, welt, whale, wheat, whole, wombat, wore, worm, worth, wrath, wreath

Puzzle 43: Word Search—Elijah

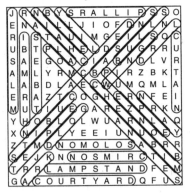

Puzzle 44: Sneaky Words—Bible Critters II

1. Well, I'll be a roadrunner's uncle!
2. "Don't you dare pick my pocket," said the kangaroo sternly.
3. I prefer my corn on the cob rather than cut into a dish.
4. Those sweet little burros prey on absolutely no other creature.
5. Liverwurst or kale—he'll eat anything.
6. We all abhor senseless violence.
7. Belinda the Wonder Beagle sang patriotic songs while waving a flag with her tail.
8. If you'll paint the walls aqua, I'll stick up some fish pictures.
9. The story tells how a peasant eloped with a king.
10. I must have pulled thousands of dandelions today.
11. A dishonest mouth is full of lies.
12. On such a cold day, his naked foot was turning blue.